MW00461259

HOW TO RAI$E A BABY
BILLIONAIRE

365 TIPS ON
CREATING THE MINDSET
OF A BILLIONAIRE

ANN MCNEILL

DEDICATION

This book is dedicated to

To Daniel,

My loving, smart, kind, handsome, husband. You have the largest heart for giving to children of all ages. Thanks for believing in me and inspiring me to greater things. I would not be who I am without the seeds you have sown into my life. Your love, friendship, and your unselfish giving to all of us have helped to spark the beginnings of the BabyBillionaire Mindset for our family. I love you, respect you, and admire you.

To Danelle,

Thanks for being such a wonderful daughter. You are kind, respectful, and beautiful inside and outside. Please forgive me for all the challenges we went through as we learned together how to raise a child with a BabyBillionaire Mindset. Thanks for your patience. Your gift is making room for you and you are a gift to all of us. Thanks for following your dream regardless of the cost.

To Ionnie,

Thanks for being a wonderful daughter, also and teaching the world by example what a Baby Billionaire looks like. Thanks for allowing me to experiment with you with the concept and the idea of the BabyBillionaire Mindset and teaching me, when you were only 9 years old the power and difference in promoting financial empowerment to the youth rather than financial literacy.

To Malachi,

Thanks for being an incredible grandson. You amaze all of us with your wisdom, knowledge and understanding of technology, to only be 12 years old. Thanks for teaching all of us the power of the BabyBillionaire Mindset at the tenth power when executed without hesitation. Thanks for being the first among us to become a published author at age 11. You are the BabyBillionaire of the future.

To You,

The reader, the clients, the audiences, and all who inspired, believed, and encouraged us while on this journey of raising children to have a BabyBillionaire Mindset, as we teach them to have a better quality of life, in every area of their lives.

ACKNOWLEDGMENTS

I am grateful for the people whose paths cross mine and whose lives make mine richer, more joyful, and more successful. This book has been a 15 year long process of walking the talk, then coming to the realization that there was a need to create a process of the BabyBillionaire mindset philosophy, utilizing the principles of Napoleon Hill's book, Think and Grow Rich. I am especially thankful to the following people for their hand in opening doors along my path that enable me to grow and share divinely inspired wisdom with those who are open to listening.

My sincere appreciation to:

My husband, Daniel McNeill, Thank you for being caring and supportive of our entire family through the good and the bad times, while we travelled and learned how to invest in ourselves, in the process of building this philosophy.

Our children, Thank you Danelle and Ionnie McNeill, and our grandson Malachi Munroe, for allowing me to experiment with the ideas, processes, and the systems, of raising children who at an early age were focused on goal setting and goal achivement.

My parents, Lucius and Alberta Cobb. My father gave me the work ethic to work like it all depends on me and my mom gave me the faith to believe like it all depends on God.

My clients, readers, and audiences, for encouraging and inspiring me through your feedback, gratitude, success stories, and questions. May this book give you the tools to raise your children with the BabyBillionaire mindset.

A very special thanks to the entire team of volunteers of the South East Chapter of the National Association of Investors Corporation (Better Investing). The training on investing and how to analyze a stock gave Ionnie and myself the foundation for this philosophy while she was 7 years old attending classes with me. Great gratitude is owed to the volunteer instructors Ellis and David Traub, Irving Roth, Phil Keating, Dr. Barbara Cobb, Lewis Adrian, Patricia Edwards, and all of the women of our Staff Investment Club.

Thanks to all my friends of the International Mastermind Association family and founders:

Isabella Rivers, Dr. Mia Y. Merritt, Nifretta Thomas, Juanita Dawsey, Lawanda Scott, Tanya Jackson, Gail Seay, Alice Fincher, Lynn Whitfield, Sherrie Harris, Carolyn Williams, and Sherree Cunningham. Thanks for prayers and encouragement along this new and exciting journey. Thank your from the bottom of my heart. You have all sown seeds into my life that is producing a tremendous harvest. Thank you for believing in me.

Thanks Palm Beach Life Planners Mastermind Group; Sharon Jackson, Stephanie Eubanks, Dr. Bettye Knighton, Laura Grier, Mariama Williams, Doretha Dennis, for having me as a member and holding me accountable for completing this manuscript.

Marily, a retired, IBM Executive, for your continuous encouragement for me to write the book and share the philosophy with the world.

The entire Emerge Publishing team, for the spirit with which you publisish this and all of your books. What a pleasure and a blessing to work with you.

Bishop Victor T. Curry, for the inspiring examples you set and the tremendous spiritual growth we have experienced in your church and through your ministry.

Thanks to.....

Ashley Justice for helping me to write the first draft.

Marilyn Johnson for encouraging me for years to write the book

Most important, I thank God for using me as a vessel to deliver words of inspiration, truth, and a proven system of how to raise children with a BabyBillionaire mindset.

CONTENTS

INTRODUCTION

What is a Baby Billionaire?

A baby billionaire is a young person at heart who has chosen certain values in their life to live by. They have decided to have a dream, then work to have that dream come true. Then they have decided to leave a legacy by which other Baby Billionaires can do the same.

The foundation of a Baby Billionaire Mindset philosophy comes down to this: Teaching our youth to save and invest in every area of their lives. As it relates to our children, consider the power of compounding of your time and your money. You can create this mindset and then create any life you want for them. No matter how difficult it may seem, by understanding how small, positive steps and actions will make a big difference over time. It's the things you do every day that don't seem to matter... they do matter most to children. In this book, you'll find through the Baby Billionaire Mindset tips that will teach how to invest in every area of your children's life.

Once you begin to use these tips on a regular basis and they become habits, you will come to understand that small investments of time and money over a long period of time will yield great results. Little things do matter. The choices you make are important. You must have a dream to have a dream come true, starting with your dream for your children.

We are all born with the ability to succeed, to live a life of prosperity in every area of our life, especially financial success. But this will only happen if we develop and nurture our lives the way we develop our thinking for ourselves, our loved ones, and especially our children.

Over the last three decades I have watched and guided students, individuals, and families in making life choices. I have sought to understand and influence what will help each person find a dream while achieving financial security and success in life. The children we are given in life are often determined by factors beyond our control, but it is what we decide to do with the children that matters most. And that is determined by our investment of time in the area of ourselves, specifically investing in our children and the values we teach them. Children who are to achieve their dream need a framework they can rely on. That framework is often times directly tied to our dream for ourselves or for them.

"As children think, so are they. ~Based on Proverbs 23:7

To collect your free gift worth $17.00, send an email to tips@annmcneill.com

To create the Baby Billionaire Mindset Spirituality starts with the end in mind.

What greater foundation can we give our children over and above a spiritual foundation that helps them understand the power of prayer, praise, and worship of a higher power than themselves, as it relates to everything in their lives? What a way to start to invest in them while they are young and to teach many values at the same time.

1 **Pray with your child daily...**Spend some time in worship with your child each day before leaving home.

2 **Tell the story...**Make sure your child understands the history of his faith.

3 **Take time to really listen...**Make sure that you stop whatever you are doing, give your undivided attention, and give solid answers when your child asks questions. Let him know that he is your priority.

4 **Read the Bible...**Set aside a day for reading together and alone.

5 **Encourage her to keep a prayer journal...** Writing her prayers will help her realize how God is working in her life.

6 Share your testimony with your child... Knowing the results of your struggles may help her through her own.

7 Teach her to be open to blessings...Remind her that some things must be accepted on faith.

8 Encourage relationships with friends who share your faith...Children and teens often lack support from close friends concerning spiritual matters.

9 Remind your child of your spiritual values when opportunities arise...If she knows how you might react, her moral compass will be strengthened.

10 Encourage a spiritual attitude toward dating... Remind her that connecting spiritually is important as she seeks a future mate.

11 Exemplify your spiritual values in your relationship with your spouse...She will expect nothing less or more from her future relationships than what she sees in yours.

12 Weekly attend religious studies together... Encourage education in your faith.

13 Connect with a leader in your faith...He or she can serve as a mentor and answer more difficult questions about spirituality and faith as well.

14 Encourage fellowship...Instill the importance of gathering with people of similar faith.

15 Tell her often that faith is important...She will trust your beliefs.

16 Get her involved in local missions and church work...Allow her to experience the good that can be done for others through faith and works.

17 Live an example of a faith driven life...Let her see your commitment to your religious convictions on a daily basis and live your life on purpose.

18 Encourage religious reflection...It will help her better understand her own spiritual needs.

19 Explain the parallels of stewardship in life and finance...Teach her that she is accountable for both.

20 Help her get to know her spiritual gifts... Explain that her God-given talents can be used if she is willing to use them.

21 Post a scripture or thought each day...A simple note of faith on your fridge will give her something to look forward to–especially when changed daily.

22 Research faith-based questions together... Learning together will strengthen the bond and the faith you share.

23 Offer thanks at meals...Make meal time a scheduled time for prayer.

24 Bring on the rain...Explain difficult experiences will make him stronger and help him create a closer relationship with the Almighty.

25 Encourage memorizing Scripture from the Bible or a book that offers great advice...It will help her know the material better and she'll be able to draw on that knowledge later.

26 Help her list her blessings...She will realize she is blessed when she realizes how many good things are in her life.

27 **Send him on a youth retreat with your church or synagogue...**These trips will help him feel a closer bond with God.

28 **Teach him to read other books on faith...** Additional reading will help strengthen his faith.

29 **Encourage quite time in prayer alone...**Allow her to spend one-on-one time with her Creator. Teach your child to pray about everything.

30 **Teach her the real meanings of the holidays you celebrate...**Christmas is more than Santa and Easter is more than a bunny. Whatever holidays you celebrate, make sure she understands the meaning behind the secularized version she sees on TV.

31 **Ask her tough questions...**Give her the opportunity to examine her religious convictions.

32 **Participate in praise activities together...**She'll be more comfortable in praise if she knows that you are doing the same.

33 Let your own involvement at your church or synagogue be an example...Your child will realize the worth of the work you are doing.

34 Encourage your child to lead in worship... Suggest he use his talents in music, drama, or speaking to participate in a religious service.

35 Explain other religious ceremonies and traditions...Tell your child what you know of religious ceremonies and traditions that are not part of your own religious background.

36 Teach your child about other religions... It will help her become stronger in her faith.

37 Encourage respect...Let your child know that you expect them to treat those of other faiths well.

38 Make grace a part of your lives...Determine times when you'll extend grace for less than perfect behavior on your child's part and make sure he understands that grace was indeed extended to him.

39 Teach forgiveness...Forgiving is as much for your child as her foe; encourage her to let go.

40 Provide a gratitude journal and encourage them to write in it every day....

41 Discuss times of healing and prosperity... Share stories from your personal experiences that are a result of your relationship with God.

42 Encourage daily family devotional time... Discuss life lessons and spirituality together as a family.

43 Pray for guidance...and raise your child according to what guidance you're given from God.

NOTES:

What are your child's spiritual goals? Please write them below.

_____

_____

_____

FAMILY

"The family that talks together stays together." ~ *Marva Collins*

To collect your free gift worth $17.00, send an email to tips@annmcneill.com

The power of a family is often in the foundation we build for our children. Our children are an extremely important part of our family and we should let them know that. The success includes, but not limited to, creating a family main statement together. It should include making and keeping promises and teaching family values. Our greatest joys and deepest heartaches surround what is happening in our family life. In every family the spirit of grandparents is very important and the role they play in the development and success of raising children with a Baby Billionaire Mindset. Learning together can be a powerful force in a family, so if possible read the book together and discuss the activities as a family, make changes, whatever you do, star now.

44 **Spend time together...**Schedule it on your calendar weekly or monthly to have some fun with your child one-on-one. A separate time is a great time to teach basic principles of life.

45 **Tell her who she's like...**If she reminds you of a dear family member, let her know.

46 **Expect respect...**Encourage her to treat all members of the family with dignity.

47 Put family first...Remind her that family time takes precedence over time with friends at times.

48 Engage her friends...Include her friends in your family activities whenever possible. It will be good for your child and those you include.

49 Create a family mission statement together... This will become the guiding light for the family.

50 Encourage your child to read books on how to strengthen the family...Reading is important.

51 Form a family investment club...Make this a weekly time to share while learning and earning together.

52 Introduce your child to relatives who have passed away...Pull out the photo albums and tell him all you know about the relatives in those pictures.

53 Help your child create and send out a family newsletter once each year...Family members will appreciate it and your child will get to know more about each of them.

54 **Create a family tree...**so that your child knows where he comes from and can research interesting ancestors.

55 **Keep a calendar that chronicles everyone in your home's activities...**Explain why respect dictates that some activities take precedence over others.

56 **Gather at the dinner table...**Spend meal time each evening discussing the good and bad things that have happened today and how to make tomorrow better.

57 **Insist on family time...**Make sure your child remains grounded by being reminded of her roots and spending quality time with family.

58 **Chronicle memories...**Begin a family scrapbook to detail important moments in your life as a family.

59 **Encourage great relationships with siblings...**Someday, they may be one another's only family.

60 **Tell good stories...**Talk about your youth and memorable family events.

61 Keep extended family close...Use email and internet to communicate with those who don't live close by.

62 Talk about family roles...Explain the responsibilities and expectations of all family members to your child, including his own.

63 Be the sort of parent you want your child to emulate...She will grow up to be a lot like you.

64 Create family traditions in your own home... Your child will treasure these memories for a lifetime.

65 Follow the family traditions of her grandparents...It will help her understand them better, even if she doesn't spend much time with them because of distance or illness.

66 Take her to work...She will better appreciate how you provide for her if she's seen you in action.

67 Acknowledge family each night...Even if only for a few minutes before bed, come together as a family and say goodnight.

68 Send her to stay with relatives...Allow her to spend time with family members who can add perspective to her image of your family unit.

69 Give her some space...If she shares a room with her sibling, give her a place to be alone.

70 Listen to your child...Listen empathetically before you attempt to explain yourself, while showing unconditional love.

NOTES:

What are your child's family goals? Please write them below.

_____

_____

_____

"The first step in changing any behavior is to start immediately." ~William James

To collect your free gift worth $17.00, send an email to <u>tips@annmcneill.com</u>

Developing a Baby Billionaire Mindset does not just happen in the lives of our children. This requires daily deposits of time. Every deposit you make with your child provides an armor against the wrong hands, which awaits them in the real world. Your child can never become overdrawn if you make the right deposits daily. Consider the return on your investment of time over time.

71 **Save to invest...**Start saving in a piggy bank. Then use the savings to purchase a share of stock, This will help your child to begin a small portfolio.

72 **Teach the difference between needs and wants...**Help your child differentiate what he may desire from what is really necessary.

73 **Teach your child about interest...**Tell her how it can help if she saves and hurts if she borrows.

74 **Play savings games...**Encourage her to save every $1 bill she receives in change or to do the same with cash of another denomination.

75 **Don't hand out cash for every outing...**If your child uses her own money, she will naturally spend less.

76 Encourage her to build an emergency fund...Teach her to save a portion of her earnings for unforeseen events.

77 Teach him to pay bills on time...This saves money on late fees, and alleviates stress.

78 Teach him to invest early...Investing early can make MILLIONS in difference later on.

79 Teach her to leave invested money invested...Withdrawing it only hurts the bottom line years later; long-term investments can help build wealth.

80 Encourage the use of a debit card, rather than a credit card...Explain that using plastic means using real money, and credit card purchases must be paid back.

81 Study the power of inventing together...Teach your child what you know about investing and be ready to learn the power of investing by learning together by taking Better Investing classes.

82 **Encourage spending...**When your child makes a profit, encourage her to reinvest a portion and enjoy a portion of the proceeds by buying something she wants.

83 **Be transparent...**If your child asks about how you've fared in handling money, be honest and recount both your successes and the areas in which you've learned valuable lessons.

84 **Give money to a good cause...**Set an example of philanthropy.

85 **Help your child prioritize...**Children's activities are expensive and can be overwhelming for the children themselves when there are too many going on. Set a budget for extracurricular activities and help your child choose how to spend their dollars.

86 **Become members of an investment education organization** like Better Investing – www.betterinvesting.org.

87 **Encourage good record keeping...**Have him keep a journal of what he spends—and why.

88 Teach your child the dangers of credit... Discuss in detail the consequences of not being able to pay back monies borrowed.

89 Teach frugality...Encourage shopping for the best deals, saving money, and choosing alternatives to expensive brand name products.

90 Encourage your child to teach another...Ask your child to share what she knows about investing with a peer.

91 Monitor her bank account...Ask questions if you aren't sure of her spending habits.

92 Teach basic money management...Your child should know how to write a check, balance a checkbook, and make a deposit from early in life. Teach how money works and its purpose.

93 Use a salesman to your advantage...Seek out a broker or financial advisor who is willing to answer investment questions for your child.

94 Show excitement...Be positive and express pride when your child shows an interest in investing.

95 Encourage bargain hunting...Help her look for similar items that cost less when making a purchase.

96 Teach smart shopping...Teach her not to buy unnecessary items just because they are on sale.

97 Choose weekly or monthly topics to learn more about with your child...Consider stocks, bonds, mutual funds, certificates of deposit, exchange traded funds, etc.

98 Play investment games...Seek out games and contests wherein you child can build a mock portfolio, buy and sell securities, and gauge how well he might have done if he invested real money.

99 Encourage research...Help your child find out more about the security in which she's considering an investment. If a mutual fund, what is the company's history? If a multi-security fund, what is the investment strategy of the fund manager and how has it fared in the past?

100 **Have her read the fine print...**When opening a financial account, teach your child to look for hidden fees and other charges and to make well informed decisions concerning those matters.

101 **Align investing with your child's interest....** Help her buy stock in her favorite companies based on the toys, clothes, and food she likes.

102 **Encourage budgeting...**Help your child determine how to spread the money she earns and is given.

103 **Examine financial statements with your child...**Make sure he understands what is going on with his investments and why.

104 **Introduce her to a trusted financial advisor...** Seek out someone who can help her make solid investment decisions.

105 **Talk openly about risk...**Some stocks and bonds are safer than others. Make sure your child understands the concept of risk in investing and how risks can be tempered with diversification.

106 **Help him diversify...**Encourage your child to choose investments that span a wide array of options, and don't put all your eggs in one basket.

107 **Discourage unnecessary spending...**Help him make good buying decisions.

108 **Introduce the concept of inflation...**Explain that a dollar today is worth more than a dollar tomorrow, and that investing can offset the value we lose to inflation.

109 **Take breaks when necessary...**If your child resists learning about a new financial topic, or shows little interest in a concept you introduce, take a brief break from the content or change topics altogether. You can always revisit information later when your child may be more receptive.

110 **Teach the value of money...**Does your child know how much groceries cost? How much minimum wage is? The cost of a new pair of sneakers? Make sure he is aware of what things cost and what it takes to earn enough money to buy them.

111   Begin to fund your child's retirement early... Help your child to learn the power of compound interest for his retirement-yes, retirement.

112   Allow a rare splurge...Let you child buy something he truly wants occasionally to avoid spendthrift rebellion later.

113   Give her an allowance...and have her pay some sort of expense from it weekly.

114   Encourage her to save for college...Part of her income from allowance or a job should be earmarked for education.

115   Be the custodian of your child's brokerage account, if he has one...and oversee his investment decisions, securing advice from a financial advisor when possible.

116   Help her create a budget...and help her understand how to use and adjust

NOTES:

What are your child's financial goals? Please write
them below.

_____

_____

_____

"Reading makes a ready man." ~ *Francis Bacon*

To collect your free gift worth $17.00, send an email to tips@annmcneill.com

Educationally, when building the mindset of a Baby Billionaire, consistency and repetition are the key. Information that has not been caught has not been thoroughly taught. Continue to offer the value of reading books. When investing in their education the library and Google are their best friends. How often are you asked a question by your child which can be answered in the library or by teaching them how to properly use Google to find answers? For example, ask your child which college they would like to attend. Choose 3 to 4 and use this exercise as a research game to review the qualifications to help them set goals. Help them understand what it takes to get admitted with scholarships.

117 Use car time wisely...Create games that emphasize skills such as math or reading, also utilize this time to read aloud and discuss topics such as newspaper headlines, books, articles, etc.

118 Set information to music...Singing the lesson in a song will help her remember.

119 Tout education...Remind your child regularly the value of education. Encourage schooling after high school graduation and explain the benefits of a college degree.

120 **Let her do it herself...**As tempting as it may be to complete a school project for her, remember learning comes from action and experience.

121 **Research careers early...**Make sure your child is aware of his employment options after graduation and the financial risk and benefits associated with his choices.

122 **Have your child complete aptitude tests...** Measure and encourage her academic strengths.

123 **Encourage her to consider the promise of her degree...**She should honestly ask herself if a rewarding career will be awaiting her after graduation.

124 **Apply for college scholarships and grants...** Not doing so is leaving money on the table.

125 **Expose your child to life on campus...**Let her spend some time eating in a cafeteria or staying overnight in a dorm if the opportunity arises.

126 **Advocate extracurricular learning...**Teach her that she can learn lots outside the classroom.

127 Teach her to make study guides...Have her organize information for tests so that it is easy to study.

128 Encourage involvement in academic societies...These will look great when she applies to college and will give her something to take pride in.

129 Check up on your child's academic progress... Ask about your child's work at school.

130 Attend parent-teacher conferences...Meet with teachers and ask them to provide their insight into your child, his attitude, and his academic accomplishments.

131 Know which academic programs are available to your child...Know what classes are offered and help him make good choices.

132 Check nightly to ensure that homework is complete...School work should be a priority.

133 Know her limits...be reasonable about your academic demands.

134 Quiz your child before the big test...Helping him study will instill confidence.

135 Reward her for exceptional grades...If she does well, recognize the accomplishment with something material that she wants.

136 Use competition to your advantage...Propose a contest with siblings to see who can make the most progress toward academic goals.

137 Keep lines of communication open with educators...Give teachers and principals your number and encourage them to use it.

138 Teach her the alphabet forwards and backwards...A fun skill, it will help her think outside the box.

139 Encourage her favorite subject...Buy books and attend exhibits that pertain to areas of study she enjoys.

140 Encourage the study of a second language very early...This will prepare your child for the future.

141 Reiterate the importance of great grammar... Discourage incorrect writing

142 Neatness counts...Teach her that educators should never receive sloppy work.

143 Make sure his mental math skills are developed...Your child needs to know how to calculate change for major denominations of currency mentally.

144 Encourage extra credit projects...If he is inclined to go above and beyond academically, let him know you're proud of that.

145 Help your child begin a personal portfolio for college...Include artwork, writing samples, and journals from science fair projects.

146 Teach her to outline...Staying organized as she writes papers and takes notes in class will be a benefit later.

147 Hire a tutor...When academics are especially tough, call for help.

148 Ensure that tardiness is never an issue...Get her to school on time, every time.

149 Teach her to make flashcards...Use index cards and write questions or terms on one side and the answers or definition on the other so that she can quiz herself before a test.

150 Visit a local college campus...Allow her to ask questions of an admissions person or student guide.

151 "Adopt" a non-local college student at your church...Ask him to dinner and offer a place to do laundry in exchange for your telling your child more about college life.

152 Encourage your child to speak with a trusted professional about how important education is...The same advice you give may be better received from a party who is not as close to your child.

NOTES:

What are your child's educational goals? Please write them below.

_____

_____

_____

HEALTH

"Trust thyself. Every heart vibrates to that iron string." ~Ralph Waldo Emerson

To collect your free gift worth $17.00, send an email to tips@annmcneill.com

When creating the Billionaire Baby Mindset in the health area consider the fact that their health is their wealth. When was the last time you made a deposit in your child's emotional and physical bank account? The words you say can impact your child equally or greater than the food they eat. Would you consider starving your child? Well, isn't that what we do when we don't give them kind words of praise every now and then?

Consider our own health habits and our children will model the same. If we are overweight and have unhealthy eating habits we are investing in the same mindset for our children. Remember they are like video recorders. Everything counts and the recorder is always on. We are always taping lessons for our children. This video recorder allows for no excuses. What you type is what your child will hear and live. If you want your child to be healthy and develop healthy living habits it starts with you. Record properly or be ready to watch your own negative tape played back by your child in later years.

153 Encourage regular exercise...Stress that a healthy body will allow him to do more and feel better.

154 Encourage a healthy breakfast...Make sure she goes to school with fuel for learning.

155 Provide healthy snacks...Remember that good food is important for both body and mind.

156 Encourage stretching...Remind your child to begin each morning with a stretching routine to prepare her body for the day ahead.

157 Require personal cleanliness from an early age...Cleanliness is considered next to Godliness for a reason.

158 Encourage down time...Allow your child to rest and rejuvenate regularly.

159 Insist on at least eight hours of sleep nightly...Your growing child needs sleep for growth and development.

160 Encourage a healthy body image...Be aware of your child's concerns about her physical appearance.

161 Stress drinking water...Water keeps her hydrated and healthy and is a good habit to form.

162 Encourage healthy eating...Eat fresh fruits and vegetables as much as possible.

163 Discourage the use of tobacco...Teach your child the deadly effects of this too common drug.

164 Teach moderation...Let your child know that some things are not good when consumed in great amounts: these include alcohols, sugars, starches, and fats.

165 Schedule regular dental visits...Teach your child the importance of dental health early and she will keep up good habits throughout life.

166 Encourage team sports...It will build character and teach him to work with others.

167 Take long walks together...It will give you time to talk about his day and is good for you both physically.

168 Seek the advice of a physician...If your child is ill or you aren't sure how to handle a health related issue, ask your family doctor.

169 Have a family doctor you love...If your child grows up with the same physician, she will be more comfortable confiding in him.

170 Keep the school informed...If she needs medications or even a little coddling, let teachers and administrators know why she isn't at her best.

171 Keep first-aid supplies on hand...You never know when you might need a band-aid, an icepack, etc.

172 Keep a phone nearby as often as possible... Cell phones are handy, especially in emergencies.

173 Train your child for health emergencies... Make sure he knows where to go or who to call if the worse occurs

174 Teach the proper hand-washing technique... Clean hands keep your child healthy and therefore more focused.

175 Give lots of TLC...When your child is ill, tender loving care is often the best medicine.

176 Keep the chicken soup stocked...It really does have healing abilities for miseries such as the common cold.

177 Keep vitamin supplements on hand... Especially if you know there are foods he won't try.

178 Have her vision screened annually...Don't take for granted that she can see clearly.

179 Keep him home when he's ill...Don't expose a sick child to others.

180 Answer personal health questions openly...Be honest no matter how difficult the subject.

181 Don't give him too much information... Answer only those health-related questions he asks so that you don't overwhelm him.

182 Don't accept too many excuses...Children will often play sick for sympathy. If there are no signs of illness and the doctor can't put a finger on what is wrong, tell you child to stick it out.

183 Know when she's really sick...Check for symptoms of real illness when your child complains of feeling ill.

184 Know the signs of stress in your child...Call for a time out if he is overwhelmed.

185 Get to know the school nurse...She may be your first indication that your child is ill or injured.

186 Don't fuss too much over a runny nose... Sometimes illness should just run its course.

187 Keep anti-bacterial wipes handy...Kill germs at their source on shopping carts and door handles to prevent illness.

188 Bring in the troops...Have a trusted family member or friend help you deal with your child's health issue if you're too upset to think clearly in extreme situations.

NOTES:

What are your child's health goals? Please write them below.

_____

_____

_____

PROFESSIONAL/ BUSINESS CAREER

"*Success is using your talents and gifts to their highest advantage and contribution. Wealth may come with this or it may not.* ~ *Fred Smith*

The power of teaching our children to set professional goals early is very important. Consider helping your child to create an annual report for their life. Yes, an annual report. We started the Baby Billionaire annual report at age 8. No. not on purpose. This is how it looked. She decided to write an affirmation (statement sharing four major goals.

Goal #1: Spiritually, was to read her Bible daily.

Goal #2: Educationally was to get straight A's in school

Goal #3: Financially she wanted to have a lot of money.

Goal #4: Recreationally she wanted to learn to play basketball and golf.

Now to fast forward 10 years later,

Goal #1: Was achieved 60 to 70%

Goal #2: She graduated with 4.6 GPA

Goal #3: She won the scholarship for "Girls Going Places" at age 18 and she was totally vested in her retirement.

Goal #4: In high school she was captain of her basketball team (3 years state champions) and captain of her golf team.

189 **Put up a chore list...**Encourage your child to complete his responsibilitiess in your home that he must complete on a regular basis. Create an allowance based on chores you child completes.

190 Remind him of the golden rule...Do unto others as you would have them do unto you. This works as well in business as it did on the playground.

191 Arrange an internship for the summer...The experience will be worthwhile, whether or not your child finds a niche.

192 Encourage her use of contacts...When seeking employment of references, remind her that she should first contact people she knows who might have a connection to help

193 Encourage him to set career goals early... Teach him the value of goal setting in the area of careers very, very early.

194 Teach her the value of web presence...Most businesses today need a virtual presence to thrive.

195 Teach her the value of time...If she makes $20.00/hour but can outsource work for $7.00/hour, she should consider doing so.

196 Encourage great customer service...Remind her that in business, clients are to be treated well as they are invaluable.

197   Encourage her to find an occupation she loves...Then start a business at a very early age, using these skills

198   Hold her accountable...When chores aren't done, grades aren't adequate, or poor behavior becomes an issue, make sure that your child faces reasonable consequences for her actions.

199   Encourage her to participate in the community when she does or will do business...Making connections is essential

200   Set some goals...Help your child envision success in different areas of his life goals, in writing.

201   Write out an action plan...Help your child plan, step by step, how to reach her goals.

202   Bring your child along...Whenever possible, allow your child to come with you to networking events or business meetings.

203   Plan a field trip...Spend a day at the factory, corporate office, or retail location of a business in which your child has shown interest, and build your child's interest in owning a bit of the company.

204 Arrange for your child to attend a board meeting...Find a local company willing to allow her to sit in on the management strategy that helps a business run successfully.

205 Teach her about marketing products... Marketing lessons translate well to life, as well, especially when your child begins to market herself as a potential employee or team member.

206 Talk about benefits...Introduce your child to the concept of corporate benefits, even if he or she is not working yet. Explain that benefits like health and life insurance, as well as retirement plans are important considerations in determining future employment.

207 Teach business etiquette...Politeness counts in the work world.

208 Teach them a little about a lot...Make sure your child is familiar with the basic concepts of mainstream industries.

209 Help her begin a working resume...It will be a good tool when applying to part time jobs and colleges

210 Teach the value of great help...Let your child know how valuable talented staff can be.

211 Teach her that working smarter doesn't always mean working harder...Sometimes creative solutions are the perfect solution.

212 Help her make and sell something...See her through the process from beginning to end.

213 Talk about the economy...Explain what affects the economy and how individuals and businesses can play a role.

214 Teach management skills...Teach your child that managing people is an important responsibility and should not be taken lightly.

215 Teach her the important of building a strong team...Encourage great working dynamics.

216 Attend a career fair together...This will give her some perspective of what opportunities may be available after graduation.

217 Teach her how to conduct an interview... Knowing how to ask questions of others will help her prepare for her own interviews.

218 Teach him how to identify talents in others... Encourage him to look for the best in peers, employees, and his manager.

219 Teach her basic interviewing skills... Demonstrate how to answer questions professionally.

220 Teach him how to express his abilities on paper...Help him word his abilities on job applications to accurately describe his qualifications.

221 Look for public speaking opportunities in which she can take part...Speaking before a group is an important skill.

222 Allow her to get a job...It will teach responsibility and build character.

NOTES:

What are your child's professional/career/business goals?
Please write them below.

_____

_____

_____

PERSONAL DEVELOPMENT

"If there is anything that we wish to change in the child, we should first examine it and see whether it is not something that could be better changed in ourselves." ~ Carl Gustav Jung

Personally, of our lessons learned in life we may not always know what to do and sometimes when we know it we don't always do it. We have two daughters and a grandson. What we learned from the first child we were able to enhance certain parental skills with our second child. But by the time my grandson was born I was clearer about certain areas relating to affirming our children and encouraging personal growth and development in every area of our lives, especially as it relates to what's important to them or what's important to us.

223 **Encourage gratitude...**Help your child write thank you notes to those who give him gifts.

224 **Encourage Perseverance...**Teach your child not to give up.

225 **Celebrate her differences...**No child is the same, so make sure she knows why you think she's special.

226 **Encourage commitment...**Make sure your child follows through on projects.

227 **Create a vision board...**Add images and articles that will remind your child of his goals.

228 Encourage reading for pleasure...Help your child choose books she will enjoy and encourage her to read for fun.

229 Encourage fairness....Treat everyone fairly and justly.

230 Stress organization...Teach you child to track tasks and activities on a calendar, to keep belongings put away, and to make lists.

231 Invest in your child's interests...Encourage piano lessons, art classes, scouting, etc. if your child asks to participate.

232 Attend inspirational events...Take your child to see great art, listen to great music, and hear great speakers.

233 Talk about successful people...Discuss how people your child admires got where they are today and what behaviors he may want to emulate.

234 Count mistakes as learning experiences... Discuss what behaviors should be avoided to prevent similar outcomes in the future.

235 Encourage a relationship with a successful mentor...If you child admires a trusted family friend or relative, encourage her to listen closely to the advice that person gives in investing and in other matters.

236 Goal setting...Personally treat your child to set goals in every area of their life.

237 Teach the value of proper maintenance...Tell you child that if he takes good care of his car, a home, or even clothing, and maintains those things well, he will save money in the long-run in replacement cost.

238 Let her lose her temper...Give your child some leeway to relieve stress, but only in a controlled environment..

239 Help her get it under control...Make sure she knows how to express emotions appropriately.

240 Say "no"...Let him know that some things are not negotiable.

241 Say "yes"...Give in to his creative ideas occasionally and find something he is passionate about.

242 Instill a work ethic...Teach your child that hard work really does pay off.

243 Say "I have no idea"...Tell your child when you are at a loss to know what to do in a given situation.

244 Teach her how to argue...Encourage your child to defend her beliefs with knowledge of fact.

245 Teach him to know his opponent... Preparedness in competition of any kind includes knowing the strengths and weaknesses of the other party.

246 Teach him how to get organized...and monitor his activities to help him stay organized.

247 Teach time management...Keep you child on time and on schedule.

248 Teach her when to say no...Give her license to choose not to participate in activities if she has qualms about them.

249 Teach him when to say yes...Teach him to try new things and accept challenges.

250 Do not tolerate meanness...Expect your child to treat others well.

251 Be his biggest fan...Show up and support him when he accomplishes great or minor things.

252 Encourage him to reach his own conclusions...After he knows the facts, let him make his own decisions.

253 Be his parent...Remember that no matter how much you love this child, you are not his friend; you are his mother or father.

254 Establish rules...Establish consequences when he doesn't abide by those rules.

255 Teach her how to dress appropriately...She should dress casually or professionally as appropriate.

256 Teach her modesty...Your child should be encouraged to respect her own body and it should show in her attire.

257 Encourage your child to stand up for herself... Remind her that she is her best advocate.

258 **Teach her compassion...**Teach her to give to those with less and take pity on those who can do no better.

259 **Create a routine...**Children are comforted when they know what will come next.

260 **Set limits...**Make sure boundaries are known, inside you home and out.

261 **Limit text messaging...**Too much text messaging can negatively affect a child's communication skills.

262 **Teach the child the importance of manners...**Teach the child to say "Thank You" and "Please."

263 **Reward self-control...**Do something good for a child who continues to do the right things.

264 **Know his friends...**Be aware of the people who will undoubtedly influence him.

265 **Encourage thoughtful debate...**Play Devil's Advocate occasionally to keep her thinking.

266 **Ban the term, "It's not fair,"...**Tell your child that life is what she makes it.

To collect your free gift worth $17.00, send an email to tips@annmcneill.com

267 Let her make decisions...If you always have the final call, she'll wonder what she should do when it's her turn to choose.

268 Encourage living beneath his means...Teach him that savings come before purchases.

269 Tell her when she gets it wrong...She needs to know when her decisions are not good ones so that she doesn't repeat them.

270 Don't back down...Never break your own rules.

271 Love unconditionally...Know that sometimes this means loving him enough to allow him to face the consequences of his actions.

272 Help her prioritize...Keep it simple: Faith, Family, Self.

NOTES:

What are your child's personal development goals? Please write them below

_____

_____

_____

"Be civil to all, sociable to many, familiar with few, friend to one, enemy to none." ~ *Benjamin Franklin*

To collect your free gift worth $17.00, send an email to tips@annmcneill.com

The time-worn cliché states: "All work and no play make Johnny a dull boy." It may be old, but it's still true. We must balance our lives with a degree of leisure time. When life becomes hectic, it is very important that we carve out some time for recreation. We should insure that our children learn at an early age that there is a time to work and a time to play. They are equally as important. Time spent in recreation can be as simple as taking a small nap, reading a book, watching the sun rise, or a hike in the mountains. Each person can determine how he spends his down-time.

273 **Let her be a kid...**Take some time to just play each and every day.

274 **Encourage teamwork...**Working with others is seldom easy but is a skill everyone should master.

275 **Encourage sportsmanship...**Teach her to shake her opponent's hand, even if she loses.

276 **Camp, for real...**Spend some time in the great outdoors together.

277 **Spend afternoons in the park...**Soak up some sun and spend some one-on-one time biking, blading, or walking together.

278 Spend some time at a beach...There's nothing like an ocean view to help you both maintain perspective.

279 Recognize an imaginary friend...Go ahead and set another place at the table. Kids with imaginary friends are often creative, intelligent, and imaginative –all traits you want to foster.

280 Bring back family game night...Spend some time playing games at the kitchen table; make sure every member of the family is included.

281 Entertain her friends...Treat them to ice cream, pay for a movie, or invite them to dinner. You'll know better who she's hanging out with and who she's becoming.

282 Go to a theme park...Goofy characters and cotton candy are a stress-buster for any kid, you included.

283 Watch a kiddy show on TV...Enjoy a favorite show together from when she was little.

284 Get down on your knees and play with his cars or her tea set...Your baby won't be little forever.

285 **Own a family pet...**It encourages responsibility, kindness, and loyalty.

286 **Visit tourist attractions...**Make sure your child experiences the wonders of travel.

287 **Go to concerts...**Share your love for renowned musicians, or get to know her music.

288 **Send her outside...**Sunshine and fresh air are not only healthy, they will make her more independent.

289 **Play in the snow...**Bundle up, go outside, and don't miss an opportunity to build a snowman or make an angel with your child. They will appreciate the time you spent and remember it for years to come.

290 **Teach your child how to look for free activities that can be done on the weekends...**You don't need money to fill your life with wonder.

291 **Travel...**Let him know that the world is a big place and people in it are a lot alike and very different.

292 Teach her to ride a bike or roller skate...These lessons will apply as she learns to do other difficult things throughout her life.

293 Play dress up...Enjoy some time playing pretend together. It will stimulate her imagination.

294 Open your backyard to the neighborhood kids...Your child will expand his circle of friends and learn networking skills in the process.

295 Play charades...Teach her to think about what she is seeing to determine the characteristics of whatever it may be.

296 Be good spectators together...Enjoy a ballgame or race and cheer for your favorite team or athlete.

297 Encourage good, old fashioned competition... Explain that not everyone wins every time.

298 Incorporate games of trust...Utilize games that teach trust and teamwork, including those that utilize blind folds and obstacle courses.

299 Plan a treasure hunt...Make clues age appropriate and never too easy.

300 Tell her to have a great time...and allow her to attend fun functions with friends and family members, even in your absence.

301 Let her choose the games...Let her choose the agenda for recreational outings and game nights, at least occasionally.

NOTES:

What are your child's recreational goals? Please write them below.

_____

_____

_____

CIVIC

"He profits most who serves best." ~ *Rotary*

It is important that we teach our future Baby Billionaires that investing in their community is a very important element of investing in one's life. We must give first, then receive exactly what you give in the same spirit in which you gave it. Social entrepreneurship is the goal for our children. In raising a baby billionaire, civic involvement is very important to a child having a better understanding of the value of service to the community and giving back. There is no end to the good your children can do in the community when they have a clear vision of the importance of civic involvement to their destination in life.

302 **Encourage volunteering...**Encourage your child to give time to causes he or she finds worthy.

303 **Teach the value of leaving a legacy...**Teach your child the importance of leaving a legacy of service.

304 **Take field trips to local government agencies...** Teach her where these are located and what their functions are.

305 **Attend open court...**Allow her to ask questions about what she witnessed later.

306 Take your child with you every time you vote...Let her know that it is her duty to vote and it is to be taken seriously.

307 Encourage your child to understand the issues that arise in your local community... Encourage questions about current events.

308 Encourage your child to learn more about the political parties...and why she might or might not want to be associated with each of them.

309 Encourage your child to ask questions of politicians' platforms...She should know why she does or does not support a politician's agenda.

310 Take your child to a political rally...Allow her to experience the pomp and circumstance of a campaign.

311 Encourage your child to work on a campaign... She will understand the hard work that comes with running for office.

312 Help her support a cause...Encourage a passion to help with fundraising or volunteerism.

313 Discuss **current events...**Talk about what's newsworthy around the dinner table.

314 **Encourage your child to register to vote when she turns 18...**Make sure this is an opportunity she will not pass up.

315 Attend **open-forum meetings...**Encourage your child to listen to the issues and suggestions presented at school board or city council meetings.

316 **Encourage your child to be part of a youth advisory board...**Many organizations give teens a forum to express their opinions; allow her to participate in such an organization.

317 **Teach her how to identify problems and propose solutions within your community...** Making the world a better place will give her a sense of pride.

318 **Teach fundraising skills...**It's a good way to help her support an organization she values and will also teach event planning and networking skills.

319 Help your child organize an event to draw attention to an issue...The skills she uses will be of use in her future professional life.

320 Help her find a leadership position... Leadership now is training her to be a good manager in the future.

321 Educate your children about political and historical figures who have bettered the world through civic involvement...Encourage further research on these individuals.

322 Encourage him to use social networking for a cause he believes in...Children today have the world at their fingertips. Help him use social networking to support a good cause.

323 Organize a field trip to your state capital... See the goings on there and answer your child's questions.

324 Have her write a letter to a local representative...If she considers an issue important, have her voice that opinion.

325 Exemplify selflessness...Teach her that she should leave the world better than she found it.

326 Become involved in a neighborhood organization together...Civic duty hits close to home in neighborhood clean up and watch groups. Encourage your child to get involved.

327 Encourage responsible citizenry...Point out others who are doing right and wrong, regarding the community around them.

328 Teach advocacy...Encourage your child to speak for someone or something that has no real voice.

329 Encourage study of other cultures...Your child will better understand his own culture and appreciate it more, too, when he studies the cultures of others.

330 Find out about service-learning opportunities at school...These projects provide both volunteer experience and class credit. They are a real win-win.

331 Encourage long term commitment...Check in with your child about a cause in which he believes on a regular basis. Ask him what he has done of late to support that cause.

NOTES:

What are your child's civic involvement goals? Please write them below.

_____

_____

_____

CREATIVITY

"Human salvation lies in the hands of the creativity maladjusted." ~ Reverend Martin Luther King, Jr.

To collect your free gift worth $17.00, send an email to tips@annmcneill.com

Creativity is parallel thinking. Creativity is thinking differently. It is seeing new ways, new models, new alternatives to doing something. Creativity can be viewed as leaping ahead with a vision, then looking back later to understand why it happened and what steps were taken to get there. The more a child learns to create, the greater their confidence becomes. We should teach our children to ask why, when, where, and how. We should also help them find alternative ways of doing what others often declare as impossible.

332 **Encourage your child's broad range of interests early in life...**Remember that a child who is multi-talented should be given the opportunity to grow and become a well rounded individual.

333 **Limit television and video games...**Encourage your child to play and create away from any device with a screen.

334 **Provide the supplies for creativity...**Make sure your child has what he needs to draw, color, paint, or create.

335 **Display her artwork...**Make sure your child knows that you treasure what she's created.

336 Expose her to great works of art...Visit amazing museums together.

337 Expose her to the musical masters...Take her to the symphony, opera, or even a jazz club to explore musical genres.

338 Encourage variety in his musical tastes...Give him music that includes what he loves best, along with music from other cultures and genres. If he finds something he likes, find more offerings in the same category.

339 Attend school events that showcase his creativity...Be at every art show, school orchestra concert, and dramatic production in which he participates.

340 Let her get her hands dirty...If she loves to garden or work with clay, forget the pretty petticoats and give her license to get dirty.

341 Read her poetry...Poetry—no matter if it's Shakespeare or Seuss—stimulates creativity.

342 Help her write a simple song...Even the youngest children love to make up and sing fun tunes.

343 Be silly...Spend some time doing things that make no sense and achieve little – but make her laugh.

344 Have her write it all down...Have her put ideas on paper before she forgets.

345 Lose the list sometimes...Let her know that being spontaneous is alright occasionally.

346 Color outside the lines...This makes for some of the most memorable pictures.

347 Look at the clouds together...and talk about what the shapes remind him of.

348 Ask her, "What would happen if...." and listen to her answer.

349 Encourage him to try new things...and applaud him when he discovers something he loves.

350 Dance in the living room...Encourage her to find joy no matter her location.

351 Play problem solving games...Give a task, some odds and ends, and she what she can create to solve the problem.

352 Don't disregard her natural talent...If she paints, sings, or plays basketball, find ways to encourage her gift.

353 Give him some wiggle room...Don't press the issue if occasionally he doesn't want to display his talents for the world.

354 Give her a camera...Let her capture images of those things that appeal most to her.

355 Clear the kitchen table...Give her some space to create.

356 Keep a box of odds and ends...Always be prepared to encourage that creative spark.

357 Always allow time for unstructured activities...Imagine as parent how much you enjoy free time. Your kids do too.

358 Let her bake something...Find out what she prepares best.

359 Allow the child to suggest activities...They should know how to use what is available.

360 Let her create a new game...She and others will enjoy something novel that appeals to her personality.

361 Teach him the basics of sewing...Everyone should know the basics of how to use a needle and thread if only to affix the patches he wins or replace a button in an emergency.

362 Enjoy sowing and reaping together...Teach your child that what is planted can be harvested, and what is never planted will never be. Start a garden.

363 Enjoy some basic woodworking...Teach her how to swing a hammer and drive a nail and see what transpires.

364 Enjoy good mysteries together...Discuss how each of you thinks the story will end as you progress through its telling.

365 Present her with a problem...and encourage her to get creative to find a solution.

NOTES:

What are your child's creativity goals? Please write them below.

_____

_____

_____

About the Author

 Ann McNeill, better known as *"The Master Builder Building Stronger and Better Lives"* is the President/CEO of the International Mastermind Association, an organization that helps people create work/life balance through goal setting. She is also the President/CEO of MCO Construction, which is the first African American female owned construction company in State of Florida. Ann is also the founder of *'The National Association of Black Women in Construction'*. Ann is a conference speaker and has been featured in many newspapers and magazines including Success Magazine and the Miami Herald. She was also the cover story for USA Today, Black Enterprise, and ABC World News and has been featured on Channel 10. Additionally, Mrs. McNeill was honored in AT&Ts 2010 Miami-Dade County's African American History Calendar for the month of September as an outstanding African American Achiever. Ann was also the US Department of Commerce's Contractor of the Year Recipient and has a list of other outstanding achievements. Ann is also a co-host on 880 The Biz radio show called "The Business of Money". And today she is here to

speak to us on behalf of her passion as the owner of Constructively Speaking, Inc. where she speaks to help give women in the highest income producing areas clarity in their personal and business life.

Ann married her college sweetheart, Daniel McNeill, 35 years ago. She has two daughters, Danelle, the oldest is known as the "Queen of Toastmasters", and Ionnie, the youngest daughter has branded herself as "The Baby Billionaire". She has a grandson, Malachi, who has authored his first book "The ABC's of Technology".

www.annmcneill.com
www.thebabybillionaire.com
www.liltechpro.com

CPSIA information can be obtained at www.ICGtesting.com
Printed in the USA
LVOW08s0704150713

342839LV00001B/5/P